THIS BOOK BELONGS TO:

GREETINGS

Warm greetings, Kolorkicker!

THANK YOU FOR YOUR PURCHASE.
Each line art in this coloring book was originally
designed and made exclusively by our
KOLORKICK family of illustrators.

Have a colorful adventure ahead!

THANK YOU

We have more in our shops!

Search for **KOLORKICK** Coloring Books
on **AMAZON** for Paperback Book Copies

Find our **KOLORKICK** shop on **ETSY** for
Instant PDF Downloads of our books

*Please don't forget
to leave us your
thoughts & review!*

★★★★★

For more inquiries
or concerns, email us
at robert@kolorkick.com

GIVEAWAY

We have FREE coloring pages for you!

10 ORIGINAL ILLUSTRATIONS

Just sign up to our email list at:

www.kolorkick.com

Follow & Support our socials and be part of our creative community!

○ @kolorkick   #kolorkick

f facebook.com/KolorKick

👥 fb.com/groups/kolorkickers

♪ @kolorkick   #kolorkick

Printed in Great Britain
by Amazon